The Adventures of Agent Keva: Service Dog

by

Anastasia Bluebird

DORRANCE PUBLISHING CO
EST. 1920
PITTSBURGH, PENNSYLVANIA 15238

Dorrance Publishing Co
585 Alpha Drive
Pittsburgh, PA 15238
Visit our website at www.dorrancebookstore.com

ISBN: 979-8-88729-457-5
eISBN: 979-8-88729-957-0

One day, Keva was sad her owner that she helped for many years died.

SiGH

She did not know what she was going to do. She just laid on her pillow.

Then one day, there was a knock at the door and the voice said, "I am here to see Keva."

The lady said, "Great, I am Sara, and it is nice to meet you."

Keva heard the new voice say, "Nice to meet you, my name is Anastasia." Sara explained that Keva had been sad since her owner died.

Anastasia said, "Well, maybe I can help," and she came over to Keva, sat on the floor next to her, and began to pet her. She said, "Keva, I could really use your help."

Keva looked up, became overly excited, and wagged her tail. "Oh," said Anastasia, "I see you like to help. Well, I need a service dog to help me. Do you think you would want to help me?"

Suddenly, Keva jumped up and said, "Woof woof." Keva thought, "I am so happy to help her."

So then, Anastasia said, "Come Keva, let's go," and they went outside. Keva saw the car and said, "Woof woof." Anastasia opened the door and said, "Let us go." Suddenly, Keva jumped in the car and off we drove.

On the way home, Anastasia asked Keva, "Would you like a cheeseburger?" So, they stopped to get a cheese-burger and shared it. It was love at first cheeseburger.

THE END